GOD'S BIG PROMISES

Bible Heroes

Over **60** reusable stickers

thegoodbook
for children

God's Big Promises Bible Heroes Sticker Book | © The Good Book Company 2023

thegoodbook.com | thegoodbook.co.uk | thegoodbook.com.au | thegoodbook.co.nz | thegoodbook.co.in

Written by Carl Laferton | Illustrations by Jennifer Davison | Design and Art Direction by André Parker

ISBN: 9781784988999 | JOB-007289 | Printed in Turkey

Noah Builds an Ark

Noah loved God and wanted to live under his rule. God told him that he was sending a flood to cover the earth. He told him to build a huge boat and take his family and some of every animal inside. God promised to keep Noah safe. So Noah built an ark.

Trace the words to finish the sentence:

Noah Loved God so Noah obeyed God.

God sent rain that fell for forty days and covered the whole earth. Noah's boat was the only thing left. Then God made the waters go down and told Noah to come out. God promised he would never flood the world again, and he put a rainbow in the sky to remind people of his promises.

Complete the rainbow:
1 Red
2 Orange **3** Yellow **4** Green
5 Blue **6** Indigo **7** Violet

1 2 3 4 5 6 7

Moses Leads God's People to Freedom

1. The king of Egypt had made God's people work as slaves.

Draw a sad face

2. God told Moses to lead his people out of Egypt. God sent ten plagues. The king let the people go free.

Draw a happy face

3. The king was cross that he had let God's people go. He wanted his slaves back! So he chased them with his army.

Find the angry face sticker

4. The army was chasing God's people. In front of them was the Red Sea. They were trapped. They were terrified!

Find the scared face sticker

5. God told Moses to hold out his staff. He parted the sea into two water-walls. His people walked along the dry path between them. Then the water-walls collapsed. God's people were safe!

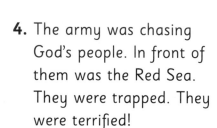

Find the path for the people to walk through the sea to safety

God's people sang to God: "There is no one like you. No one else can do what you do."

God spoke to Moses. He gave him the Ten Commandments so that his people would know how to obey him.

Samson Dies to Rescue God's People

God gave Samson great strength. Find the stickers of things that Samson could lift:

Deliliah knew that if she cut Samson's hair, he would lose his strength. So she cut it. The enemies of God's people put him in prison.

CRASH!

Samson's hair started to grow again. When his enemies brought him out to laugh at him, he prayed and pushed the pillars of the building.

Samson was crushed – and so were his enemies. He had rescued God's people!

Find these words from the story of Samson:

- ☐ strong
- ☐ cut
- ☐ hair
- ☐ push
- ☐ crash

c	r	a	s	h	g	i	p
r	f	s	a	k	n	t	u
m	s	t	r	o	n	g	s
z	t	h	a	l	e	g	h
b	h	a	i	r	x	j	p
o	a	t	a	e	c	l	o
d	i	a	d	y	u	m	a
j	t	e	r	q	t	u	t

Use the code to fill in the letters and find out why Samson was a hero.

- ⬡ = p
- ★ = e
- ▲ = l
- ◆ = d
- ■ = r
- ● = s
- ⬠ = c
- ✶ = o

Sam _ _ n
    ● ✶

_ _ _ _ _ u _ _
■ ★ ● ⬠   ★ ◆

G _ _ ' _
  ✶ ◆   ●

_ _ _ _ _ _
⬡ ★ ✶ ⬠ ▲ ★

Ruth Chooses to Join God's People

Ruth was from Moab. People in Moab did not love or obey God. When Ruth's husband died, her husband's mother, Naomi, wanted to go to Israel, where God's people lived. "I will go with you," said Ruth. "From now on, I will love and obey the God who you love and obey."

Help Naomi and Ruth get to Bethlehem:

GOD'S **BIG** PROMISES

Bible
Heroes

Ruth went to a field to pick corn for her and Naomi to eat. There she met Boaz. They got married and had a baby. Ruth loved being part of God's people.

Draw Ruth's baby, Obed:

King David Rules God's People

God decided to give his people the king they needed, who would look after them and lead them to love and obey God.

God sent his messenger Samuel to Jesse's house. He told Samuel that he had chosen Jesse's youngest son, David, to be the king. Samuel poured oil over David's head to show that he would be the king.

David looked after God's people by defeating their giant enemy, Goliath. He knocked him down with a stone from his sling.

David wrote lots of songs about God, called psalms.

David showed God's people how to obey God.

When David made mistakes, he said sorry and asked God to forgive him.

King David

ruled God's people.

Jonah Tells People about God

God told Jonah to go to the city of Nineveh. But Jonah got on a boat to run away. God sent a big storm and Jonah was thrown into the sea. Then God sent a big fish to swallow him. Inside the fish, Jonah thanked God for rescuing him. After the fish spat Jonah onto dry land, he went to Nineveh and told the people there the truth about God. They said sorry for not living his way, and God forgave them.

Start with 1 and number the boxes to put the story in order.

1

Start with 1 and join the dots to finish the picture.

Use the code to find out what Jonah did in Nineveh...

- ● = t
- ⬟ = h
- ★ = o
- ⭐ = e
- ■ = r
- ◆ = n
- ▲ = l

J _ _ a _
  ★ ◆   ⬟

     d
_ _ _   _ _ _
● ★ ▲   ● ⬟ ★

    u
_ _   _ _
● ■   ● ⬟

Esther is Brave

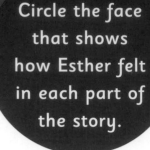

Circle the face that shows how Esther felt in each part of the story.

Esther was one of God's people. King Xerxes chose her to be Queen of Persia.

The king's chief servant was called Haman. He came up with a plan to get rid of all God's people.

Esther was not allowed to speak to the king without being invited. But she knew she needed to tell him about Haman's plan. Esther was brave. She went to see him...

The king listened to Esther. He got rid of Haman. God's people were safe because Esther had been brave!

Can you find these words from the story of Esther?

- ☐ esther
- ☐ plan
- ☐ king
- ☐ brave
- ☐ safe

y	k	i	n	g	g	i	o
r	f	s	s	k	n	e	u
m	b	r	a	v	e	s	t
z	t	h	f	l	e	t	h
b	g	a	e	r	x	h	p
o	a	t	a	e	c	e	o
d	p	l	a	n	u	r	a
r	t	e	r	q	t	u	h

Jesus Is the Greatest Hero

Every hero in the Old Testament part of the Bible tells us something about the greatest hero in the Bible – **Jesus!**

Jesus led God's people to freedom – like **Moses**

Jesus rescued God's people – like **Samson**

Jesus obeyed God – like **Noah**

Jesus chose to live as part of God's people – like **Ruth**

Jesus was brave – like **Esther**

Jesus is the King who rules God's people – like **David**

Jesus told the truth about God – like **Jonah**

Jesus is the greatest hero!

Draw a face to show how you feel about Jesus: